# Mediterranean Diet Recipes

Quick and Easy Cookbook to Burn Fat, Fix your Wrong Habits and Boost your Metabolism.
Delicious Meal Prep for a Healthy Lifestyle.

Tania Frei

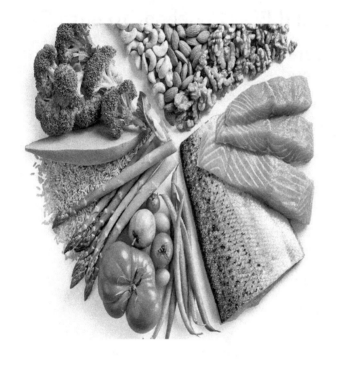

# TABLE OF CONTENTS

# CHAPTER 1

# Mediterranean lunch recipes

## Garden fresh omelets

### Ingredients

- 1 ⅓ cups of coarsely chopped tomatoes, drain
- 1 cup of roughly chopped, pitted cucumber
- Half a ripe avocado, halved, seeded, peeled and chopped
- ½ cup of roughly chopped red onion (1 medium)

- 1 clove of garlic, chopped
- Cut 2 tablespoons of fresh parsley
- 2 tablespoons of red wine vinegar
- 1 tablespoon of olive oil
- 2 eggs
- 1½ cups of chilled or frozen egg product, thawed
- ¼ cup of water
- 1 tablespoon of sliced fresh oregano or 1 teaspoon of dried oregano, crushed
- ¼ teaspoon of salt
- ¼ teaspoon of ground black pepper
- ⅛ teaspoon of crushed red pepper
- ¼ cup crumbled, reduced-fat feta cheese

## Preparation

1. For salsa, stir tomatoes, cucumber, avocado, onion, garlic, parsley, vinegar and 1 teaspoon of oil together in a medium bowl.

2. Whisk the eggs, egg product, water, oregano, salt, black pepper together in a medium bowl and crush the red pepper. For each omelet, heat 1/2 teaspoon of the remaining oil over medium heat in an8-inch non-stick skillet. Skillet with 1/2 cup of the egg mixture. Stir the eggs with a spatula until the mixture looks like fried bits of an egg surrounded by liquid. Stop stirring, but continue to cook until you set the egg. 1/3 cup of salsa spoon over one side of the egg mixture fried. Remove

---

omelet from skillet; fold overfilling. Repeat to make a total of four omelets.

3. Serve per omelet with one-fourth of the salsa leftover. Sprinkle on 1 tablespoon of feta cheese with each omelet.

# Mediterranean chicken panini

## Ingredients

- Olive oil non-stick cooking spray
- 2 small skinless, boneless chicken breasts (approx. 8 ounces in total)
- ⅓ cup of dried tomatoes (not oil-packed)
- 3 tablespoons of boiling water
- ⅓ Drain the cup of roasted red pepper in a bottle
- 4 teaspoons of balsamic vinegar
- 1 teaspoon of sliced fresh oregano or 1/2 teaspoon of dried oregano, crushed
- 1 large clove of garlic, chopped
- ⅛ teaspoon of ground black pepper
- 4 mini squares of wholemeal bagel bread or multigrain ciabatta rolls, divided
- 1 small zucchini

## Preparations

1. Coat an unheated panini grid gently, covered indoor electric grill, or large non-stick skillet with non-stick spray cooking. Preheat to medium heat or heat, as regulated by the manufacturer. Stir in the chicken. Close the lid and grill for 6 to 7 minutes when using griddle or grill, or until chicken is no longer pink. (When using a skillet, cook chicken for 10 to 12 minutes or until chicken is no longer pink, turn once.) Cool the chicken slightly;

divide each piece of chicken in half horizontally and cut into 2-inch wide slices crosswise.

2. Combine dried tomatoes with boiling water in a small pot. Cover and let 5 minutes stand. Transfer undrained tomato mixture to a small food processor (if you have a larger food processor, you will occasionally have to stop and scrape the sides down). Attach roasted red sweet peppers, oregano, balsamic vinegar, big clove garlic, and ground black pepper. Cover and work smoothly before.

3. Place the dried tomato-pepper place over cut sides of squares of bagel bread. Place the chicken on the bread squares underneath. Cut very thin strips from the zucchini using a vegetable peeler. Layer slices of zucchini on top of the chicken. Place the tops of the square bagel on top of the zucchini, spread sides down. Click gently. Coat each sandwich lightly with nonstick cooking spray at the top and bottom.

4. Put sandwiches on board, grill, or skillet, if necessary attach in batches. Open the lid and grill for 2 to 3 minutes or until bread is toasted, if using griddle or grill. (If you use a skillet, place a heavy saucepan or skillet on top of the sandwiches. Cook for 1 to 2 minutes or until the bottoms are toasted. Carefully remove the saucepan or top skillet; it can be hot. Flip the sandwiches; cover with the saucepan or skillet again. Cook 1 to 2 minutes longer or until the bread is toasted.)

---

# Spinach Stuffed Mushrooms

## Ingredient

- 16 oz white whole mushrooms or "crimini."
- 3 crushed garlic cloves
- ¼ cup onion, minced
- ¼ cup white wine or vegetable stock
- 3 tablespoon low sodium soy sauce or tamari
- 3 cups sweet spinach
- ¼ cup white beans
- 2 tablespoons nutritional yeast
- ¼ red pepper, minced

## Preparation

1. Preheat the oven to 375 degrees F.
2. Remove the stems from the mushrooms, leave the tops intact and chop the stems.
3. Sauté the onion, garlic, and mushroom stalks in a pan.
4. Add the wine and the soy sauce or tamari, continue cooking for 2-3 minutes, or until the vegetables soften a little.
5. Add the tender spinach and sauté for a minute.
6. move the vegetable mixture to a food processor.
7. Add beans and nutritional yeast and mix to combine.
8. Transfer to a bowl and mix the chopped red pepper.
9. Place the mushroom tops with the top side down in a baking dish.

10. Fill each mushroom top with the mixture.

11. Bake for 20-25 minutes.

12. Remove from oven and serve hot

## Crispy Cauliflower Chips

### Preparation
- Ahead of cauliflower, cut into florets
- ½ teaspoon garlic powder
- ½ teaspoon of seasoning for poultry or seasoning without salt (optional)
- ¾ cup of aquafaba
- 1 cup gluten-free bread crumbs

### Preparation
1. Preheat the oven to 450 degrees F.
2. Put the cauliflower in a container and season with the garlic powder and the seasoning for birds (or without salt). Be sure to cover the cauliflower evenly.
3. Soak the cauliflower, a foil at once, in the aquafaba, and shake off the excess.
4. Cover with breadcrumbs and shake off excess.
5. Repeat with all cauliflower florets.
6. put the florets on a baking sheet lined with baking paper.
7. Bake for 15 minutes.
8. Turn the florets over to bake evenly.
9. Bake for another 15 minutes.
10. Serve immediately.

# Baked potatoes without oil

## Ingredient

- 4 medium yellow potatoes
- ½ teaspoon garlic powder
- sea salt and pepper to taste

## preparations

1. Preheat the oven to 400 degrees F (218 degrees C).
2. Cut the potatoes into sticks similar to "fries" of approximately ½ "- ¾" thick.
3. Put the potatoes in a deep pot, cover with water, and boil for 5 minutes.
4. Drain well and pour it into a deep container.
5. Add the spices and cover the potatoes well with the seasoning.
6. Put the potatoes on a baking sheet covered with a silicone foil or baking paper.
7. Bake for 35-40 minutes or until cooked and crispy. Enjoy your meal!

# Red cranberry and kale pilaf

## Ingredient

- 1 cup of brown rice
- 1 ¾ cups vegetable stock
- 1 small yellow onion, diced
- 12 ounces (340 grams) of kale (approximately 5 cups)
- 3 or 4 cloves garlic, minced
- ½ teaspoon red pepper flakes
- ½ cup dried cranberries
- ¼ cup chopped cashews or other nuts (optional)

## Preparation

1. In a medium-sized pot or rice cooker, cook the rice in the broth according to package directions.
2. Sauté the onion for five minutes, or until it is transparent.
3. Add the kale (without stems and thickly chopped leaves) and cook for another five minutes, or until the kale is soft.
4. Add the garlic in flakes and red pepper and cook everything for another minute.
5. Add the cooked rice and continue sautéing for three minutes, or until the rice has completely warmed.
6. Remove the pan from the heat.
7. Add red cranberries and optional nuts, stir well.

# Sweet potato tropical casserole

## Ingredient

- 4 cups diced sweet potatoes
- 1 cup diced mango
- 1 cup diced pineapple
- ½ teaspoon unsalted garlic and herb seasoning
- ½ cup pineapple and coconut juice

## Process

1. Preheat oven to 350 degrees F.
2. Combine all ingredients in an 8 x 11 (2 qt) baking sheet.
3. Bake covered for 25 minutes.
4. Bake uncovered for 5 minutes and serve.

# Traditional stuffing

## Ingredient

- ½ cup vegetable broth
- 1 spoon low sodium soy sauce or tamari
- 4 cups gluten-free or whole-wheat bread cubes
- ½ cup chopped onion
- 1 cup chopped celery
- 1 tablespoon nutritional yeast
- ½ teaspoon bird seasoning
- ½ teaspoon garlic powder
- ½ teaspoon dried parsley

## Process

1. Preheat the oven to 350 F.
2. In a small bowl, mix the soil flax seeds with the water and set aside for 10 minutes.
3. In a big bowl, combine every dry ingredient.
4. Cut and place the apples in thin slices in a container.
5. Add the pumpkin puree, vanilla extract, water-based flaxseed, and apple date paste and blend well.
6. Combine the dry ingredients and blend well with the apples. If the mixture tends to be too dry, add water.
7. In an appropriate baking dish, put the mixture and bake for 30-35 minutes.

# Quinoa Pilaf Stuffing

## Ingredient

- ½ teaspoon sage
- 1 teaspoon thyme
- 1 teaspoon rosemary
- ½ cup wild rice
- 1 ½ cups quinoa
- 1 cup brown rice or rice mix
- ½ cup freshly squeezed orange juice
- 2 ½ cups of vegetable stock
- ½ sea salt
- 1 cup grated carrots
- 1 cup pomegranate seeds (optional)
- 1 cup gooseberries (optional)

## Process

1. Heat a pot over medium heat.
2. Add the spices to the pot and sauté for 30 seconds.
3. Add wild rice, quinoa, and brown rice and stir for 1 minute.
4. Add orange juice, vegetable broth, and sea salt, and stir well.
5. Bring to a boil, cover and reduce heat to medium-low and cook for 45 minutes.
6. Remove from heat, add carrots and fruit, and serve.

# Mashed sweet potato with cauliflower

## Ingredient

- 1 head of cauliflower, without the core and cut into pieces
- 2 large sweet potatoes, peeled and cut into pieces of 1 inch (2.5 centimeters)
- ½ cup unsweetened vegetable milk
- 1 teaspoon garlic powder
- Salt and pepper to taste

## Process

1. Steam the cauliflower and sweet potato in approximately 1-2 inches (2.5 - 5 centimeters) of water until soft. Alternatively, you can roast them on parchment paper in the oven at 400 ° F (204 ° C) for 20 to 30 minutes.

2. Add the soft vegetables to your food processor and process everything for one minute to dissolve the ingredients, or you can crush them by hand. Add the vegetable milk, garlic powder, salt, and pepper and continue processing until smooth.

# Brussels sprouts caramelized with blueberries.

## Ingredient

- 8 chopped dates
- ½ cup of water
- 3 cups fresh Brussels sprouts, cut in half
- 1 cup fresh blueberries
- 1 tablespoon miso paste
- 1 cup low-sodium vegetable broth or water
- 1 organic red onion, chopped
- 1 tablespoon soy sauce
- ¼ cup of nuts such as almonds, Brazil nuts, several mixed, etc. (optional) Pepper to taste

## Process

1. In a food processor, mix dates with ½ cup of water until a creamy texture is obtained. Set it aside for a moment.
2. In a saucepan over medium-high heat sauté the Brussels sprouts along with the onion, miso, blueberries and ½ cup of broth or water. Cook covered for 10 minutes or until lightly brown.
3. Stir frequently and add the rest of the additional liquid as necessary to prevent burning.
4. Cook the sprouts until they are caramelized by the edges.
5. Add the soy sauce, ground pepper, and date paste. Mix and match well.
6. Serve and garnish with nuts.

# Mediterranean chicken with 4 kinds of cheese

Chicken breasts with tomato sauce with lemon peel and a variety of cheeses are served with screw noodles.

## Ingredients

- 4 portions
- 4 halves boneless and skinless small breasts
- 1 can diced tomatoes
- 1/2 cup chopped black olives
- 1 tbsp grated lemon peel
- 1 cup five kinds of cheese finely, shredded, five cheese and blend
- In some supermarkets they all come in a bag

## Steps

15 minutes

1. The breasts are fried in little oil for 7 minutes on each side, or until cooked.
2. Add the diced tomatoes, grated lemon peel and cook for 5 minutes.
3. This mixture is added to the chicken and it is taken to the fire for 2 minutes until everything has been well mixed, and finally the cheeses are put.
4. It is served with a screw paste and is also sprinkled with tomato sauce.

# Mediterranean beef casserole

## Ingredients

6 portions

- 900 gr aguayo steak (round steak palomilla) diced
- 2 tbsp Butter
- 1 can 340 grams of tomato paste
- 2/3 cup beef broth or red wine
- 1/2 cup sliced black olives
- 2 tbsp light brown light sugar
- 2 teeth chopped the garlic
- 1/4 cup red wine vinegar
- 2 leaves laurel
- 1/4 cup grapes
- 1 cdts ground cinnamon
- 1 cdts ground clove
- 3 cups hot steamed rice

## process

50 minutes

- Preheat the oven to 375 F in a bowl, mix the steak, the melted butter settles in a baking dish.
- Mix in a bowl the tomato paste, the meat broth, the vinegar, add stirring the olives, sugar, garlic, pour over the steak. Turning it to spread it.

- Put the bay leaves on top of the meat mixture; distribute the raisins, cinnamon, cloves, cover with aluminum foil.
- Bake the casserole for 45 minutes, take out the bay leaves, discard them, arrange the cooked rice in a serving dish and on the rice, spread the meat and the sauce by spoonfuls.

# Mediterranean rolls

## Ingredients

4 portions

- 1 sliced eggplant
- 1 tbsp cheese
- 1 1/2 tbsp chia of
- 5 oz cream cheese
- 1/2 roasted pepper cut into brunoise
- 1cda post or fresh basil
- for in dressing:
- 1/2 tbsp white vinegar, olive oil to taste a touch of pesto
- salt and pepper to taste (the ingredients are mixed and olive oil is added in the form of thread until emulsified)

## process

30 minutes

- The eggplant is cut into thin slices and grilled until softened.
- Mix the cheese, pepper, and basil, Parmesan cheese with mayonnaise mix everything, wrap this mixture with the eggplant slices and then add the dressing on top.
- Note: eggplants are put a decorative stick to hold. If you want you can take them to the oven but it is optional.

# Mediterranean fish fillet

## Ingredients

2 portions

- 2 steaks fish (Huauchinango, Robalo, Snapper, sea bream, etc.)
- 1-2 tomatoes
- 1 can mashed tomato
- black olives needed
- 1-2 teeth Garlic
- parsley
- Salt
- Pepper
- 1 Pope
- olive oil

## process

30 minutes

- In a saucepan, we put olive oil and a clove of garlic chopped to brown when the aroma releases, add one or two peeled and chopped tomatoes, then add tomato puree, season with salt and pepper and add a peeled and diced potato 1 cm., we add some olives and chopped parsley. When the potatoes have been cooked, carefully place the fish fillets that are cooked over low heat, if necessary add a little water.

- Serve them with white rice.

## Baked fish Mediterranean style

### Ingredients

- 1 steak fish per person
- 3 chambray onions
- 1 tooth garlic for each steak
- red onion or échalots
- Salt
- Pepper
- dill powder
- olive oil
- Butter
- capers (optional)
- two lemons

### process

20 minutes

- In a refractory we place our fish fillets on a little olive oil, and we put them on top: each: salt and pepper, a clove of minced garlic, chopped red onion or eschalots, the tails of about 3 small onions of chopped chambray and the onions are cut in half and placed on the sides, dill powder, a few capers, the juice of a lemon, olive oil and a piece of butter on top of each.

- It is put in a hot oven and you have to be on the lookout because it should not be more than 8 or 10 minutes so that it does not dry out, when we take it out we decorate the fillets with lemon slices.

# Beef Meatballs in Vegetable Bath

## Ingredients

6 portions

- 1/2 Bell pepper
- 1/2 stem celery
- 3 teeth natural garlic
- 3 teeth roasted garlic
- Chicken broth to liquefy the seasonings
- 4 ripe tomatoes
- 1 tbsp Mediterranean oil (canola-grape seeds-Extra virgin olive) to saute the seasoning
- 14 Large beef meatballs (baseball ball size)
- 16 oz of tomatoes in pieces with their juice
- 1 pinch ground turmeric
- 1 pinch ground cumin
- 1 tsp ground onion
- 16 ounces cooked and drained chickpeas
- Chicken broth as required.
- 1 cup carrots on thick wheels
- 6 pieces 1 baseball-size potato
- 1 cup peeled and chunky Aoyama

## process

70 minutes

- Process the seasoning (the first 6 ingredients) and the tomatoes, in the blender covering with liquid chicken broth.

- In the pot you will prepare the broth, pour the oil and saute the liquefied seasoning.

- Add the meatballs, use pre-cooked and frozen. This speeds up the preparation process. Continue to soften and unite.

- Then add the carrot, chicken broth (I used broth prepared at home) but you can use the one you like. Add water to get the desired consistency. The Aoyama in pieces. Potatoes in large pieces. The can of tomato and the chickpeas drained.

- Add the Curcuma and cumin, after tasting taste.

- Reduce heat and cook until vegetables are tender.

- When extinguishing the fire add a sprig of thyme and oregano, preferably natural. Cover and let stand for 10 minutes before serving.

- It depends on the meat and personal taste, the fat is removed using a fat separator or allowing cooling because the fat floats on top and so you remove it.

- Accompany with white rice or bread

## Burritos of Cabbage

### Ingredients

- One green or Chinese cabbage (12 leaves)
- 300 g ground beef
- One outing
- One clove of garlic
- 400 ml diced tomatoes
- One tablespoon tomato puree
- One tablespoon of taco herbs
- One small can of corn
- Two hands of grated cheese
- 100 gr kidney beans from a sack

### Preparation

1. Chop the onion and then garlic and fry in a pan. Add the minced meat and then the taco herbs. Bake this loose. Stir in the tomato puree and cubes and then the drained corn and kidney beans. Let this burrito filling simmer for a few minutes. Meanwhile, boil water.

2. Heat the oven to 180 degrees. Cut the cabbage leaves and boil them (per 2 or 3) for a minute or 2 in the pan and then drain well. Place two cabbage leaves next to each other so that they overlap slightly. Spoon some of the burrito filling on one side, sprinkle with a little cheese and then carefully roll-up. Don't push too hard. Repeat this with the rest of the cabbage leaves and filling. If they

are all in the baking dish, sprinkle them with some extra cheese. Put the baking dish in the oven for about 15 minutes. Serve the carbohydrates with some rice (if the dish is no longer low in carbohydrates).

# Black Bean and Quinoa Burgers

## Ingredient

- 3 cups cooked black beans
- 1 cup cooked quinoa
- 1 cup flaked oatmeal
- 2 tablespoons ground flaxseed
- ½ cup barbecue sauce
- ½ teaspoon of liquid smoke or smoked paprika
- 1 teaspoon garlic powder
- ½ teaspoon onion powder

Additional barbecue sauce for hamburger

## Preparations

1. Preheat the oven to 400F.
2. Partially pest the beans.
3. include the rest of the ingredients and mix well.
4. Shape the burgers with your hands compacting well.
5. Put the burgers on a baking sheet covered with baking paper.
6. Bake the hamburgers for 15 minutes.
7. Flip the burgers and cover with a layer of barbecue sauce.
8. Bake for 10-15 more minutes.

# Roasted Cauliflower with Turmeric

## Ingredient

- 1 large cauliflower
- 2 teaspoons finely grated fresh ginger
- 1 tablespoon tahini
- 1 tablespoon organic miso paste, non-GMO
- 3 tablespoons vegetable stock
- 3 prunes or dates, chopped
- ½ teaspoon of turmeric powder
- 2 tablespoons tamari
- Ground black pepper, to taste
- Black and white sesame seeds, to decorate
- Sliced green onion, to decorate (optional)

## Preparation

1. Preheat the oven to 425 degrees F.
2. Cut the leaves and stem at the bottom of the head of the cauliflower, so that it is flat.
3. Click with a sharp blade so that the spices penetrate the cauliflower.
4. Remove the cauliflower from the oven and sprinkle the top with one of the green onions (optional), the tamari, a pinch of ground black pepper, and sesame seeds before serving.
5. Mix the ginger, tahini, miso paste, broth, prums or dates, and turmeric in a food processor.

6. Rub the paste over the cauliflower using your hands, ensuring that it is spread everywhere, even at the edges.

7. In the oven, roast the cauliflower for 45 minutes or until golden is soft and cool.

# Creamy mushroom lasagna, gluten-free

## Ingredient

- 3 cloves garlic, ground
- 16 ounces of chopped champignons (you can use a mixture of different champignons)
- 1 tablespoon of tamari or aminos (amino acids in liquid, in Spanish) of coconut or soy sauce, gluten-free
- 1 teaspoon dried thyme
- Thirty-four cup raw cashews, soaked for a few hours, drained overnight.
- 1 cup vegetable broth + a little more to saute garlic and mushrooms
- 2 large handfuls of spinach
- 10 ounces of lasagna sheets, gluten-free (I love Tinkyada brown rice pasta)
- 4 cups marinara sauce, purchased at the store (a 32 oz or 946 ml bottle) or homemade
- Nutritional Yeast (optional)

## Preparations

1. In a skillet, heat a little vegetable stock at medium temperature. When it is hot, add the garlic and skip it until it releases the aroma. This will take a minute. Add the mushrooms, tamari (or coconut or soy amino sauce, gluten-free), and thyme. Cook, mix more or less every

minute, for six or eight minutes or until the mushrooms release their water, and a small broth begins to form.

2. Combine cashews and vegetable broth in a high-speed blender and blend until the mixture is completely uniform. This may take five minutes, depending on your blender's speed and power. Verse the cashew sauce with the mushrooms in the pan. Reduce heat to medium-low and simmer to let the sauce thicken, stirring frequently.

3. make the lasagna sheets according to the package instructions. Be sure to do this after your mushroom sauce is ready so that the slices do not remain static for a long time and begin to stick. Spread a third of the marinara sauce in the bottom of a baking sheet eight to eleven inches in size (20 to 28 cm). Add a layer of sheets. Cover them with half the mushroom cream. Add a layer of sheets. Use another third of the marinara sauce to cover them. Add the remaining mushroom cream. Add the last layer of sheets and cover them with the remaining marinara sauce.

4. Cover the lasagna with foil and bake for 30 minutes. Remove the paper, add some nutritional yeast on top, if you want, and cook it for another 15 minutes. Let the lasagna stand for five minutes before serving.

## Traditional Greek salad

### Ingredients

- 2 tomatoes
- Cucumber
- 3 small red onions
- A handful of green and black olives
- 25 dag feta
- 2-3 tablespoons of wine vinegar
- 6 tablespoons olive oil
- 2 tablespoons oregano
- Salt
- pepper

### How to prepare the recipe:

1. Peel cucumbers and onions, wash tomatoes. Dice tomatoes and cucumbers, and onions into rings. Mix the vegetables . Cut the feta
into cubes, add to vegetables along with olives.

2. We prepare the sauce: mix the oil with wine vinegar, season with salt and pepper. We pour the salad. We sprinkle with oregano.

# Tomato and feta salad

## Ingredients

- 2 tablespoons of balsamic vinegar
- 1/ 2 teaspoons of chopped fresh basil or 1/2 teaspoon of dried basil
- 1/2 teaspoon of salt
- 1/2 cup of roughly chopped sweet onion
- 1 pound grape or cherry tomatoes, halved
- 2 tablespoons of olive oil
- 1/4 cup crumbled feta cheese

## Directions

1   Mix vinegar, basil and salt in a large bowl. Add onion; throw to coat. Let it rest for 5 minutes. Add the tomatoes, oil and feta; throw to coat. Serve with a slotted spoon.

# Colourful layered salad

## Ingredients

- iceberg lettuce
- tomatoes
- ¾ cans of corn
- medium cucumbers
- yellow pepper
- 2-3 red onions
- chicken breasts (about 0.5 kg)
- seasoning for peas and chicken
- 2-3 pieces of bread
- seasoning for toasts
- Butter and oil for frying
- Herb sauce

## How to prepare the recipe:

1. Cut the chicken into small pieces, sprinkle with gyros and chicken, the season in the fridge for 1-2 hours.
2. Layer the salad in layers. We tear the lettuce and put the dishes on the bottom. Cut the tomatoes into halves or slices. We drain the corn. Peel cucumbers and cut into halves or slices. Then cut the peppers into strips. Cut the red onions into quarters of the slices.
3. We heat oil and fry chicken.

4. Cut the bread into small cubes, warm up the butter in a pan and pour the sliced bread on them. Fry until golden brown, sprinkle with a toast to the end of frying.

5. We prepare herbal sauce according to the recipe on the packaging and pour the whole salad before serving.

## Nopal Soup

### What you will need

- 2 pounds of nopales, clean and diced
- 4 Roma tomatoes
- ¼ white onion
- 2 cloves of garlic
- 1 chipotle chili in adobo (optional)
- 3 cups of vegetable stock
- 1 tablespoon dried oregano
- Salt and pepper to taste

### *OPTIONAL COVERAGES*

- Avocado
- Coriander
- Chives
- Lemon or Lime Juice

### Preparation

1. Cook the nopales for 20-25 minutes in boiling water with salt or until they lose their bright color and are tender to bit.
2. Place the tomatoes, onion, garlic, and chipotle in a blender glass. Blend until you get a creamy consistency.
3. Remove the nopales from the heat, drain them, and rinse them with enough cold water. Leave aside.
4. In a pot, sauté the tomato sauce for about 3 minutes.

5. Add cooked nopales and oregano to tomato broth. Let cook another 15 minutes.
6. add salt and pepper to taste.
7. Serve on soup plates and add toppings.

## Matzo Ball Soup

### What you will need

*MATZO BALLS*

- 1 ½ cups quinoa flakes
- 1 ½ cups of mixture gluten purpose flour
- 2 teaspoons onion powder
- 1 teaspoon garlic powder
- ¼ teaspoon of sea salt
- 2 cups of boiling water
- 6 tablespoons pumpkin puree

*SOUP*

- 1 medium yellow onion, chopped
- ¼ cup of Coconut Aminos
- ½ teaspoon freshly ground black pepper
- 5 medium carrots, peeled and sliced
- 3 celery stalks, diced
- 2 parsnips, peeled and sliced
- 1 cup fresh parsley, chopped
- 8 cups of vegetable broth without sodium

*COVER*

- 3 tablespoons fresh dill, finely chopped

### Preparation

1. Preheat the oven to 200-300 degrees F (148 ° C). Cover a 15 x 13 inch (38 x 33 cm) baking sheet with parchment paper.

2. To make matzo balls: Beat quinoa flakes, flour, onion powder, garlic powder, and salt in a medium bowl. Add the boiling water and the pumpkin and stir to combine.

3. Take at least a tablespoon of the mixture and form a ball. Place the ball on the prepared baking sheet. Repeat until you have used the entire mixture. You should have approximately 30 balls.

4. Bake the matzo balls until they are a light golden color, approximately 20 minutes. Turn the balls halfway through cooking.

5. Transfer the baking sheet from the oven to a wire rack and let it stand for 10 minutes.

6. To make the soup: heat the onion in a large pot over medium heat and stir until it begins to release its aroma, approximately for a minute.

7. Add the Coconut Aminos, black pepper, carrots, celery, parsnips, and parsley and cook, stirring occasionally, until the vegetables release their aroma and are slightly soft, about two minutes. Add the broth and boil.

8. Reduce the heat intensity, cover the pot, and let simmer for about 35 minutes.

9. Serve immediately and place several matzo balls in each bowl of soup. Sprinkle dill in the soup.

10. The soup tastes even better the next day, and even better two days later.

# CHAPTER 2

# Mediterranean dinner recipes

**Mediterranean Baked Cod Recipe with Lemon and Garlic**

### Ingredients

- 1.5-pound cod fillet pieces (4-6 pieces)
- 5 garlic cloves, peeled and minced
- 1/4 cup chopped fresh parsley leaves
- 5 tablespoons of fresh lemon juice
- 5 tablespoons of private extra virgin olive oil

- tablespoons of melted butter
- 1/3 cup all-purpose flour
- 1 teaspoon of coriander powder
- 3/4 teaspoons of Spanish sweet pepper
- 3/4 teaspoon ground cumin
- 3/4 teaspoons of salt
- 1/2 teaspoon black pepper

## Preparation

1  Preheat the oven to 400 F.

2  In a shallow bowl, combine the lemon juice, olive oil and melted butter. Set aside Mix flour, spices, salt and pepper for all uses in another shallow bowl. Put the mixture next to the lemon juice.

3  Dry fish fillet with pat. Dip the fish in a lemon juice mixture, then dip it in a flour mixture. Shake off excess flour.

4  Heat 2 tablespoons of olive oil over medium-high heat in a cast-iron skillet (look at the oil to make sure it is sizzling but not smoky). Add fish and sear on each side to give it some color, but don't cook completely (about a few minutes on each side) Remove from heat.

5  Attach the minced garlic to the remaining lemon juice mixture and blend. Drizzle the fish fillets all over.

6  Bake until it starts to flake easily with a fork in the heated oven (10 minutes should be finished, but start checking earlier). Remove the chopped parsley from heat and sprinkle with it.

7   Serving suggestions: Serve with Lebanese rice and this Mediterranean chickpea salad or the popular Greek immediately

## Chicken Shawarma

### Ingredients

- 3/4 tablespoons ground cumin
- 3/4 tablespoons of turmeric powder
- 3/4 tablespoons of coriander powder
- 3/4 tablespoons of garlic powder
- 3/4 tablespoons of paprika
- 1/2 teaspoon of ground cloves
- 1/2 teaspoon cayenne pepper, more if you prefer
- salt
- boneless and skinless chicken legs
- 1 large onion, thinly sliced
- 1 large lemon, juice of
- 1/3 cup private extra virgin olive oil reserve
- 6 pita pockets
- Tahini sauce or Greek tzatziki sauce
- rocket salad
- ingredients of Mediterranean salad
- Pickled olives or Kalamata (optional)

### Preparation

1 Mix the cumin, turmeric, coriander, garlic powder, sweet paprika and cloves together in a small bowl. Place the shawarma spice blend aside for now.

2 Pat the chicken thighs on both sides, dry and season with salt, then slice thinly into small pieces of bite-size.

3   Place the chicken inside a big bowl. Remove the spices of shwarma, and toss to coat. Add the onions, the juice of the lemon and the butter. Again throw all together. Cover and cool for 3 hours or overnight (if you have no time, you can cut or miss the marinating time)

4   Preheat the oven to 425 degrees F when they are ready. Take out the chicken from the fridge and let it sit for a few minutes at room temperature.

5   Spread the marinated chicken over a large, lightly oiled baking sheet pan with the onions in one layer. Roast the 425 degrees F heated-oven for 30 minutes. Moves the pan to the top rack and broil very quickly (watch carefully) for a more browned, crispier chicken. Remove from the frying pan.

6   Prepare the pita pockets whilst the chicken roasts. Create tahini sauce as per this recipe, or Tzatziki sauce as per this recipe. Create the Mediterranean salad3-ingredient according to this recipe. Deposit aside.

7   Open the pita pockets, to eat. Spread a little tahini or tzatziki sauce, add chicken shawarma, arugula, Mediterranean salad and, if you like, pickles or olives. Eat straight away!

# Moroccan vegetable tagine recipe

## Ingredients

- 1/4 cup of Riserva extra virgin olive oil, more for later
- medium yellow onions, peeled and chopped
- 8-10 cloves of garlic, peeled and chopped
- large carrots, peeled and chopped
- 2 large red potatoes, peeled and diced
- 1 large sweet potato, peeled and diced
- sale
- 1 tablespoon of a mixture of Harissa species
- 1 tablespoon of coriander powder
- 1 teaspoon ground cinnamon
- 1/2 teaspoon turmeric powder
- 2 cups canned whole peeled tomatoes
- 1/2 cup chopped dried apricot
- 1 liter of low sodium vegetable broth (or broth of your choice)
- 2 days of cooked chickpeas
- 1 lime, juice of
- A handful of fresco parsley leaves

## Preparation

1   Heat olive oil over medium heat in a large heavy bowl, or Dutch Oven, until shimmering. Add the onions, and heat up to medium-high. Saute for 5 minutes, tossing periodically.

2   Remove all the chopped veggies and the garlic. Season with herbs and salt. Toss to merge.

3   Cook on medium-high heat for 5 to 7 minutes, and mix frequently with a wooden spoon.

4   Garnish with onions, apricot and broth. Spice with a slight dash of salt once more.

5   Keep over medium-high heat, and cook for 10 minutes. Reduce heat, cover and simmer for another 20 to 25 minutes or tender before veggies.

6   Stir in chickpeas and cook over low heat for another 5 minutes.

7   Incorporate lemon juice, and fresh parsley. Seasoning to taste and change, adding more salt or harissa spice mix to your liking.

8   Move to bowls for serving and finish each with a generous drizzle of extra virgin olive oil from Private Reserve. Serve hot with couscous, or pasta, your favorite meal.

# Green salad with Chicken Rey and egg

## Ingredients

- 1/2 iceberg lettuce
- 2 carrots
- 2 hard-boiled eggs
- 1 chicken breast
- 1 tomato
- Mayonnaise
- olive oil
- Pepper
- Salt

## Preparation

- Wash and cut the iceberg lettuce to Juliana. We booked in a large bowl.
- We wash and cut the tomato into dice. We add to the bowl.
- Peel and cut the carrot julienne. We add to the bowl.
- Cut the chicken breast into strips.
- Cook the eggs for 10-15 minutes in a saucepan with a stream of vinegar and salt, so that they do not break.
- When the eggs are ready, we remove, cool with a jet of water and remove the shell.
- Chop the hard-boiled eggs into quarters and add to the bowl.

- Meanwhile in a pan with a drizzle of oil, place the chicken strips, season and brown the chicken for 5 minutes over medium heat.
- Mix the salad with a couple of tablespoons of mayonnaise to taste and serve immediately.

# Panera Bread Green Goddess Cobb Salad

## Ingredients

*Pickled onions:*

- 1 cup of sliced red onion
- 1/2 cup white vinegar
- 1 tablespoon of sugar
- 1 1/2 teaspoon of salt
- 1 cup of warm water

*Salad servers:*

- 6 ounces of salad mix-use rocket, romaine, kale, and radicchio mix
- 6 ounces of grilled chicken breast
- 2 tablespoons of crispy cooked bacon
- 3 tablespoons of chopped avocado
- 1/2 cup of chopped tomatoes
- Halve 1 hard-boiled egg
- 2 tablespoons of feta
- 2 tablespoons of pickled onions

*Green goddess salad dressing:*

- 1 cup of mayonnaise
- 2 tablespoons of tarragon leaves
- 3 tablespoons of chopped chives
- 1 cup of flat-leaf parsley

- 1 cup of packed watercress cleaned and hard stems removed
- 2 tablespoons of lemon juice
- 1 tablespoon of champagne vinegar
- 1/2 teaspoon of salt
- 1/4 teaspoon of pepper

**Direction**

- Cut onions as thin as possible, I like to use the 1/8 inch setting on my mandolin. Put the onions in a jar wide. Mix white vinegar, sugar, salt and warm water in a small bowl. Stir until sugar and salt have dissolved. These should rest for about 30 minutes for use.
- Put all the ingredients for the dressing in the bowl of a blender or food processor and mix for 30-45 seconds, or until the dressing is mostly smooth and creamy.
- Place the salad on the bottom of a large salad bowl. Cut the chicken breast into thin slices and place on the salad. Add bacon, chopped avocado, chopped tomatoes, feta cheese, hard-boiled egg halves, and pickled onions. Drizzle with as much salad dressing as desired. Remaining salad dressing can be kept in an airtight container for 1 week.

## Caprese tomato, mozzarella, basil and avocado salad recipe

### Ingredients

- 2 sliced avocados
- 2 ripe tomatoes
- 500 g mozzarella cheese
- 1 cup fresh basil leaves
- 1/4 cup olive oil
- 1/4 cup balsamic Aceto
- Salt and ground black pepper

### Direction

- Gather all the ingredients to make this tomato, mozzarella, basil, and avocado Caprese salad.
- With a small knife, cut the end of the tomato stem and then, using a serrated knife, cut the tomatoes into slices.
- Cut the mozzarella into slices and see alternating slices of avocado, tomato, mozzarella and basil leaves in individual dishes.
- Sprinkle with olive oil and balsamic vinegar and season lightly with salt and ground black pepper.
- Spread your Italian tomato, mozzarella, basil and avocado salad with a fresh baguette or on a bed of romaine lettuce.

# Creamy Potato Salad

## Ingredients

- 1 kilo of potatoes
- ¾ cups of low-fat sour cream
- ¼ cup of mayonnaise
- ¼ cup chopped fresh parsley
- 3 tablespoons lemon juice
- 2 tablespoons Dijon mustard
- 2 tablespoons chopped fresh tarragon
- 2 chopped celery stalks
- 2 hard-boiled eggs
- 1 small fennel, thinly sliced

## Direction

- Peel the potatoes and cut them into medium cubes. Place them in a large pot with cold water and kosher salt to taste, and add a little salt. Bring to the fire and when it boils, simmer until the potatoes are tender 10 to 12 minutes.
- Mix mayonnaise with sour cream, mustard and lemon juice.
- Season with salt and ground black pepper and add warm potatoes. Mix and let cool to room temperature.
- Add the celery cut into thin slices as well as fennel and parsley and tarragon, all finely chopped.

- Mix so that the potatoes are impregnated with cream and add the hard-cut eggs in wedges. Serve the creamy potato salad.

**Wedge Salad with Creamy Dressing**

## Ingredients
- 1 cup Daisy Cream
- 1/2 cup skim milk
- 4 teaspoons cider vinegar
- 1 sachet of green onion powder mix
- 1 clove garlic, minced
- 1/2 cup sliced green onion
- 1 head of iceberg lettuce, removed the heart and in pictures
- 1 tomato, diced
- 4 teaspoons diced bacon

## Instructions
- In a small bowl, combine the cream, buttermilk, vinegar and dressing mix. Beat until the mixture is smooth. Add garlic and 1/4 cup green onion; set aside. Remove the center of the lettuce and cut into 4 equal wedges. Place each wedge in four different dishes. Pour about 1/4 of the salad dressing over each wedge. Distribute 1/4 of the remaining onion, 1/4 of the chopped tomato and 1 teaspoon of diced bacon on top of each wedge.

---

# Tomatoes stuffed with tuna

## Ingredients

- 2 cans of water or natural tuna
- 4 medium tomatoes
- 1 large cup of white or brown rice
- Mayonnaise c / n
- Green olives c / n
- Peas or capers c / n
- 2 carrots
- Salt c / n

## Direction

- Place plenty of water in a pot and bring it to the fire. When it boils, pour the rice. Stir with a wooden spoon so that it does not stick and cook for 20 minutes or until it is soft. Remove, drain immediately and reserve in the fridge.
- Peel the carrots and cut them into small cubes. Cook in a pot with water until they soften. Drain and place in a bowl.
- Add the rice, the two cans of drained tuna, the peas or capers (cooked) and the mayonnaise to taste.
- Mix everything very well and room to taste.
- Wash the tomatoes very well and smoke them with the help of a knife and a spoon.

- If you want to take advantage of what you have taken to the tomato, cut it into small cubes and mix it with the rice or reserve it for another recipe.
- Fill the tomatoes with the rice and the tuna. Garnish with some mayonnaise in the center and a green olive.

# Seafood paella recipe

## Ingredients

- 4 small lobster tails (6-12 ounces each)
- water
- tablespoons of extra virgin olive oil from the reserve
- 1 large yellow onion, chopped
- cups of Spanish rice or medium-grain rice, soaked in water for 15-20 minutes and then drained
- garlic cloves, minced
- 2 large pinches of Spanish saffron threads, dipped in 1/2 cup of water
- 1 teaspoon Spanish sweet pepper
- 1 teaspoon cayenne pepper
- 1/2 teaspoon of Aleppo pepper flakes
- salt
- 2 large Roma tomatoes, finely chopped
- ounces of green beans, cut
- 1 kilo of prawns or large prawns or your choice, peeled and gutted
- 1/4 cup chopped fresh parsley

## Preparation

1   Take about 3 cups of water in a large pot to a rolling boil. Attach the lobster tails and let boil until pink for a very brief time (1-2 minutes). Then turn off the heat. Attach a pair of

tongs to the lobster tails. Do not waste cooking water on the lobster. When the lobster is sufficiently cool for handling, remove the shell and break it into large chunks.

2   Heat 3 tbsp of olive oil in a large deep pan, or cast-iron skillet. Turn the heat and add the chopped onions to medium-high. Saute the onions for 2 minutes then add the rice, and cook 3 minutes more, stirring frequently. Now add cooking water for the chopped garlic and the lobster. Extract the saffron and the oil, paprika, cayenne pepper, Aleppo pepper and salt are soaking. Attach the chopped tomato and green beans. Bring to a boil and let the liquid reduce slightly, then cover (with a lid or tightly with foil) and cook for 20 minutes at low heat.

3   Uncover and scatter the shrimp over the rice, gently pressing it into the water. Add some water, if necessary. Cover for another 10 minutes and cook until the shrimp turns pink. Finally add bits of fried lobster. Turn heat off when the lobster gets warmed up. Garnish with peregrinate.

4   Serve the delicious paella with your white wine of choice.

# Spaghetti and Meatballs

## Ingredient

- 1½ cup of water
- ¾ cup of millet
- 1 small yellow onion, finely diced
- 4 cloves garlic, ground
- 1 tablespoon dried basil
- 1 teaspoon ground fennel seeds
- 1 teaspoon red pepper crushed flakes (optional)
- ¼ cup dried tomatoes, finely chopped
- ¼ cup artichoke hearts, finely chopped
- ¼ cup roasted pine nuts or walnuts, chopped into large pieces
- 1 teaspoon sea salt (optional)
- 1 pound whole-grain cereal spaghetti
- 1 jar (28 ounces or 828 ml) hot spaghetti sauce
- Fresh chopped parsley, for decorat

## Preparation

1  Preheat the oven to 375 ° F (191 ° C).

2  To make the meatballs, combine the water and millet in a small saucepan and bring the water to a boil at high temperature. Reduce it to medium-low and cook the millet until it is tender about 20 minutes. If it is not tender after

all the water is absorbed, add two or three tablespoons of water and let it cook for another five minutes.

3   While the millet is cooking, sauté the onion in a large skillet at medium-high temperature until it becomes translucent and begins to brown, approximately for five minutes. Add the garlic, basil, fennel, and red pepper flakes (if you use it) and cook for another minute. Add dried tomatoes, artichoke hearts, and nuts (if you use them) and remove the pan from the heat.

4   When the millet is ready, add it to the pan with the onion mixture, add the sea salt (if you use it) and mix well. Shape the mixture into balls using an ice cream spoon or a 1/3 cup measure and place them on nonstick baking paper.

5   Bake for like 15 minutes, turn them over and continue baking until the millet balls are lightly browned, about 15 minutes more.

6   To make the spaghetti while the meatballs are baking, cook the spaghetti according to the package instructions and drain it.

7   Transfer the cooked spaghetti to a larger tray. Top with meatballs and spaghetti sauce. Garnish with parsley and serve.

# Oatmeal Seasoned with Vegetables

## Ingredient

- 4 cups of water
- 2 cups of "cut" oatmeal (quick-cooking steel-cut oats)
- 1 teaspoon Italian spices
- ½ teaspoon Herbamare or sea salt
- 1 teaspoon garlic powder
- 1 teaspoon onion powder
- ½ cup nutritional yeast
- ¼ teaspoon turmeric powder
- 1½ cup kale or tender spinach
- ½ cup sliced mushrooms
- ¼ cup grated carrots
- ½ cup small chopped peppers

## Preparation

1. Boil the water in a saucepan.
2. Add the oatmeal and spices and lower the temperature.
3. Cook over low heat without lid for 5 to 7 minutes.
4. Add the vegetables.
5. Cover and set aside for 2 minutes.
6. Serve immediately.

# Rice with Smoked Sausages and Beer

## Ingredients

- 14 smoked beef sausage
- 3 1/2 cups raw rice
- 1/2 onion in small cubes
- 1/2 chili pepper in small cubes
- 1 tbsp crushed garlic
- 1 cube chicken soup
- 1/4 cup tomato sauce
- water to prepare rice
- 1 tbsp Mediterranean oil (olive-canola-grapeseed)

## Preparation

1   You add the oil to the pot you use; personally I prefer the quick pot for your convenience. Heat over medium heat; add the onion, bell pepper, and garlic, sauté, joining well.
2   Add the sausages, continue sautéing until they have browned the tomato sauce, and continue joining.
3   Rub the beer stream and continue joining while you jump. And you allow the alcohol to evaporate,
4   The rice, mix well and sauté for about 1 minute.
5   Add enough water to prepare the rice; this will depend on the pot you are using.
6   try salt and cook like normal rice

# CHAPTER 3

# Mediterranean dessert recipes

**Italian apple and olive oil cake**

## Ingredients

- large gala apples, peeled and chopped as finely as possible
- Orange juice for soaking apples
- cups of all-purpose flour
- 1/2 teaspoon ground cinnamon
- 1/2 teaspoon ground nutmeg
- 1 teaspoon of baking powder

- 1 teaspoon of baking powder
- 1 cup of sugar
- 1 cup of private extra virgin olive oil
- 2 large eggs
- 2/3 cup of golden raisins, immersed in hot water for 15 minutes and then draining well
- Icing sugar for dusting

## Preparations

1 Oven preheats to 350 degrees F.

2 In a cup, place the sliced apples, and add the orange juice. Just enough juice to throw in the apples and clean them so they don't shine.

3 Sift the flour, cinnamon, nutmeg, baking powder and baking powder into a large bowl. Add the sugar and extra virgin olive oil to a blender bowl with whisk for now. Remove at low temperature for 2 minutes, until all is well mixed

4 Add the eggs one by one with the mixer on and stir for another 2 minutes, until the mixture volume increases (it should be denser but still fluid).

5 With the dry ingredients in the large bowl, indent in the center of the flour mixture. Pour the wet mixture into the well (mix of sugar and olive oil). Replace with a wooden spoon until all have blended properly. It will be a thick batter (let nothing be added to loosen this).

6    Let the raisins dry absolutely soak in the bowl. And rid the excess juice of the apples. Add the raisins and apples to the batter and stir until all is well mixed with a spoon. The dough is going to be quite dense again.

7    Layer a 9-inch parchment paper cake saucepan. In the pan put a thick batter and align the top with the wooden spoon back.

8    Bake for 45 minutes at 350 ° F, or until a toothpick or wooden skewer has been inserted.

9    Keep it in the pan to cool completely. Just raise the parchment when you're done to put the cake in a tub. The powder was containing icing sugar. Alternatively heat up some dark honey (those with a sweeter tooth like this option) to serve.

## Chocolate Panna Cotta

### Ingredient

- Half a liter of special liquid cream to assemble
- 100 ml of milk
- 1 tablet of chocolate for desserts (black or milk, to your liking) of 100 gr
- A splash (25 ml) of Grand Marnier or an orange liqueur
- 100 gr of sugar (or something less, it depends on the sweetness of chocolate and your tastes)
- 6 sheets of neutral jelly or 1 sachet of powdered gelatin (10 gr)

### Preparation

1  Melt the chocolate in a water bath or in the microwave at medium power for about 5 min. We hydrate the gelatin leaves in a little water (about 10-15 min are enough).

2  Mix the cream with the melted chocolate over the heat and add the sugar, milk, and liquor, beating well so that the sugar dissolves. We must avoid getting to boil and we must not stop stirring so that lumps do not form. We also incorporate the gelatin and continue stirring until it dissolves well.

3  We fill some molds with this cream and leave in the fridge a few hours until it sets. I usually use individual silicone molds because it is easier to unmold and I like this candy more individually.

## Drunk chocolate cake with mousse and strawberries

### Ingredient

- 3 cups all-purpose gluten-free flour
- ½ cup date or coconut sugar
- 2 teaspoons baking powder
- 1 teaspoon baking soda
- ½ teaspoon of sea salt
- 6 tablespoons cocoa powder
- 4 tablespoons ground flax seeds
- 4 teaspoons vanilla extract
- 4 tablespoons unsweetened applesauce
- 2 tablespoons apple cider vinegar
- 1 cup raisins
- 2 cups of cold water

*COVERAGES*

- 8 cups fresh or thawed strawberries
- 4 cups of chocolate mousse

### Preparation

1  Preheat the oven to 350 degrees F.
2  In a large container, combine flour, sugar, baking powder, baking soda, cocoa powder, ground flaxseed (flax), and salt.
3  In a blender, mix the water and raisins well.

4   Pour the raisin water mixture into a separate bowl and combine it with the vinegar, vanilla, and applesauce.

5   Pour the wet ingredients over the dry ones and stir with a whisk until well mixed.

6   Pour the mixture into a round baking dish covered with baking paper.

7   Bake for 30 minutes.

8   Remove from the oven and wait for it to cool.

9   To assemble the drunk cake, start by spreading a layer of chocolate mousse at the bottom of a cake pie bowl, a round bowl, or a cup of personal size parfait.

10  Cover the mousse with a layer of strawberries.

11  Place a layer of cake. If you opt for a personal parfait, you can use a round cookie cutter to cut the cake.

12  Repeat steps 9-11 until you fill the bowl or cup.

13  The last layer should be chocolate and strawberry mousse.

# Crunchy quinoa bars

## Ingredients

- 4-ounce semi-sweet chocolate bars
- 1 cup of dry quinoa
- 1 tablespoon of PB2
- 1/2 teaspoon vanilla
- For the peanut butter dressing:
- spoons of water
- 1/2 tablespoons of PB2

## Preparation

1  Heat a pan with a heavy bottom over medium to high heat. Let it warm up for a couple of minutes before adding some quinoa Add 1/4 cup quinoa at once (so you'll have four batches to pop). Let it rest on the bottom of the pot, turning occasionally, until you start hearing the crackling of light, then constantly shake it for about a minute, until the explosion has slightly subsided. Be sure to take it off before it turns brown (it can happen very fast). You don't want anything but a toasted golden color Once all of your quinoa has sprouted, place it aside in a small bowl.

2  In a bowl, add the melted chocolate, quinoa, PB2 and vanilla-mix to thoroughly combine Line a baking sheet with parchment paper and spread your chocolate quinoa mixture on top: you do NOT have to scatter the mixture over the whole pan, or it will be too thin. Just the middle

form a square shape. The thickness is up to you - but in a small bowl, I made mine about 1/2 inch thick, add the peanut butter drizzle together. Sprinkle it all over the top of the chocolate and quinoa, then use a knife to shake it gently Refrigerate for at least one hour before slicing (or until it's absolutely hard). When sliced, I keep mine in the fridge, but the counter still works!

# Apple and pumpkin pie

## Ingredient

- 1 spoon ground flax seeds + 2 ½ tablespoons water (flax egg)
- ½ cup all-purpose gluten-free flour (or oatmeal)
- 1 ½ cup quick-cooking oatmeal
- 1 tablespoon baking powder
- 1 teaspoon baking soda
- 2 tablespoons pumpkin pie spice
- 1 tablespoon cinnamon
- 4 medium granny smith apples
- ½ cup date pasta
- 1 cup pumpkin puree
- 1 teaspoon vanilla extract
- ¼ cup of water (optional)

## Preparations

1 Preheat the oven to 350 degrees F.
2 Mix ground flaxseed (flax) seeds with water in a small bowl and set aside for 10 minutes.
3 Mix all dry ingredients in a large bowl.
4 Cut the apples into thin slices and place them in a container.
5 Add the pumpkin puree, vanilla extract, flaxseed with water, and date paste to apples and mix well.

6   merge the dry ingredients with the apples and mix well. Add water if the mixture seems to be too dry.

7   Place the mixture in an 8 x 11 (2 quarts) container suitable for baking and bake for 30-35 minutes.

## Blueberry muffins

### Recipe

*Dough*

- 28 g coconut flour
- 56 g butter (melted)
- 56 g of erythritol
- 3 eggs
- 5 tbsp whipped blueberries
- 1 tsp vanilla extract
- 1/2 tsp baking powder
- 1/4 tsp salt

*Topping*

- 113 g cream cheese (softened)
- 56 g butter (softened)
- 5 tbsp whipped blueberries
- 1 tbsp erythritis
- 1/2 tsp vanilla extract

### Cooking

*Dough*

1   Combine butter, eggs, erythritol, and vanilla extract.
2   Add coconut flour, baking powder, and salt. Beat until smooth.
3   Add the blueberry mixture and mix thoroughly.
4   Pour the batter into the muffin pan.
5   Bake for 30 minutes at 200 degrees.

6    Remove from the oven and cool.

## Brownie Fat Bombs

### Ingredients

- 110 g soft unsalted butter
- 30 g soft cream cheese
- 3 tbsp melted coconut oil
- ½ cup almond flour
- ⅓ cup of powdered keto sweetener to your taste
- ¼ cup unsweetened cocoa powder
- 1 tsp vanilla essence
- ⅓ cups of crushed chocolate without sugar (minimum 80% cocoa)

### Cooking

1 Put butter, cream cheese, and coconut oil in a bowl. Beat with a mixer until smooth.
2 Add almond flour, sweetener, cocoa powder and vanilla essence. Beat well until smooth.
3 Add chocolate and mix.
4 Cool the mixture for 1 hour or until solid.
5 Form balls the size of a tablespoon and place on a baking sheet with parchment.
6 Cool the balls for another 30 minutes before storing them in an airtight container in the refrigerator or freezer.

# Chocolate Custard

## Ingredients

- 310 ml unsweetened almond milk
- 310 ml oily whipped cream
- 6 egg yolks
- ⅓ cup stevia or erythritis
- 2 tsp vanilla essence
- 225 g sugar-free chocolate chips

## Cooking

1. Add all ingredients except chocolate and whipped cream to the pan. Beat well.
2. Put on low heat and stir continuously for 15 minutes until the mixture thickens.
3. Add the chocolate and mix well until all the chocolate has melted and mixed. To simplify the process, use a blender.
4. Divide the mixture into 8 servings.
5. Refrigerate for at least 4 hours or better at night.
6. Before serving, add whipped cream on top and sprinkle with grated chocolate without sugar.

# Chocolate Cake Espresso

## Recipe

- 1 cup shredded dark chocolate (minimum 80% cocoa)
- 1 1/2 tsp vanilla extract
- 1/4 tsp salt
- 1/2 cup erythritol, powdered stevia, or another keto sweetener
- 1/2 cup unsweetened cocoa powder
- 1 tbsp freshly brewed and chilled espresso
- 3 large eggs

## Cooking

1   Preheat the oven to 190 degrees and grease a round baking dish with unsalted butter. Put parchment on top and sprinkle it with a non-stick spray.

2   Put the pieces of dark chocolate in the microwave and heat for 1 minute. Stir and microwave again until the chocolate melts and becomes homogeneous.

3   Add eggs and sweetener to a large bowl. Beat with a blender or mixer at high speed for 1-2 minutes until light and foamy. Add cocoa powder and espresso, and beat until smooth.

4   Pour the batter into the pan. Smooth the top with a spatula. Bake for 18-20 minutes. Remove the cake from the oven and let it cool for 10 minutes.

5   Drag the knife along the edges of the cake to separate it from the mold. Put a large plate on the form upside down and quickly turn the cake on a plate. Remove and discard parchment paper.

6   Let the cake cool completely and refrigerate overnight. Garnish with berries if desired.

# Chocolate Orange Cupcake

## Recipe

- 1 chopped orange
- 4 eggs, protein separated from yolks
- 1/2 cup low-carb sweetener
- 192 g almond flour
- 43 g unsweetened cocoa powder
- 1 tsp baking powder
- 1/2 tsp salt

## Cooking

1   Put slices of orange in a pan and fill with water. Bring to a boil and cook for 1 hour. The orange should be soft enough to be pierced with a fork.
2   Pull out the orange and cool slightly.
3   Preheat the oven to 170 degrees.
4   Put slices of orange in a food processor and beat in mashed potatoes without lumps.
5   Add almond flour, cocoa powder, a low-carb sweetener, salt, baking powder, and egg yolks. Mix well.
6   Beat the egg whites until foam and carefully pour into the orange dough.
7   Place the dough in a greased cake pan.
8   Bake for 1 hour until cooked.

# Coconut Ice Cream with Berries

## Recipe

- 476 g butter whipped cream
- 226 g coconut milk
- 100 g of erythritol
- 3 egg yolks
- 4.93 g vanilla extract
- 155 g berries
- 40 g sugar-free coconut flakes
- 29.57 g of vodka (optional)

## Cooking

1 Heat cream and coconut milk in a saucepan over medium heat for about 3-5 minutes. Do not let the mixture boil!

2 While the cream is warming, beat the eggs, vanilla, and erythritol together.

3 Remove the cream from the heat and carefully pour it into the egg mixture. Beat until smooth.

4 Pour this mixture back into the pan over medium heat and beat for 5-10 minutes until the mixture begins to thicken slightly.

5 Remove from heat, add vodka and mix (if desired). Allow cooling.

6 Add the berries and coconut, then put the ice cream in an airtight container and place in the freezer. Take out the

container every 30 minutes and mix the ice cream thoroughly. This may take about 4-5 hours.

### Cranberry Low Carb Cookies

### Recipe

- 56 g coconut flour
- 60 g soft cream cheese
- 1 egg
- 113 g unsalted butter (soft)
- 113 g low carbohydrate erythritol
- 1 tsp vanilla extract
- 2 tsp cinnamon
- 1/2 tsp baking powder
- 1/2 tsp salt
- 110 g cranberries
- 43 g low sugar chocolate chips

### Cooking

1. Preheat the oven to 180 degrees.
2. Combine butter, cream cheese, and erythritol.
3. Add vanilla extract and egg. Beat until smooth.
4. Add coconut flour, baking powder, cinnamon, and salt, and beat until smooth.
5. Add cranberries and chocolate chips.
6. With wet hands, grab a large ball the size of a walnut and place on a baking sheet with parchment paper.

7   Press the top of the ball with your hand or the back of the spoon to shape the cookies. Repeat the process (you should get about 15 pcs.).

8   Bake for 20 minutes until solid and golden.

# Cherry and poppy seed muffins

## Ingredient
*DRY*

- 1 cup (120 g) raw buckwheat flour
- 1 ¼ cup oatmeal (155 g) oatmeal
- 2 tablespoons poppy seeds
- 2 teaspoons cinnamon
- ½ teaspoon cardamom
- 2 teaspoons baking powder

*Wet*

- 10 chopped figs
- A little more than 1 cup (260 ml) of vegetable milk, without sugar
- 2 ripe bananas
- 2 heaped tablespoons unsweetened applesauce
- 2 tablespoons peanut butter
- 1 pinch of sea salt (optional)
- ½ cup (50 g) dark chocolate (at least 70% cocoa), chopped
- 24 fresh or frozen cherries

## Preparation
1  Preheat the oven to 355 ° F (180 ° C).
2  Cut the figs and soak them in the vegetable milk for at least half an hour. If you soak them more, place them in the fridge.

3   While the figs are soaking, finely chop the chocolate and set aside. Combine all other dry ingredients in a bowl. Place the figs and milk in the blender. Add all remaining wet ingredients and mix until smooth.

4   Pour the wet mixture over the dry ingredients and mix well. Make sure there are no lumps. Now add the chopped chocolate.

5   Fill molds 12 muffins (I molds using silicone) with the mass and finally hits two cherries on each muffin.

6   Bake for 25 to 30 minutes. Let them cool a little before trying to remove them from the molds.

## Homemade granola

### Ingredient

- 3 cups flaked oatmeal
- ¼ cup chopped raw nuts
- ¼ cup raw pecans, chopped
- ¼ cup raw almonds, chopped
- ½ cup pure maple syrup
- 2 teaspoons vanilla
- 2 teaspoons cinnamon
- 1 pinch of salt (optional)

### Process

1  Preheat the oven to 250-300 ° F (149 ° C).
2  Put all ingredients in a bowl, mix well, and cover everything with maple syrup. Spread the mixture on a baking sheet or broiler pan.
3  Bake for 30-40 minutes with occasional stirring until the mixture turns brown. Move the top plate to the wire rack and let it cool completely. Refrigerate the granola in a sealed jar.

# Tofu cashew cheesecake dessert

## Ingredient

*For The Mass*

- 1 cup soaked cashews
- 6 ounces (175 g) of soft tofu
- 1 tablespoon peanut butter
- 1 small banana
- A handful of grated coconut
- 1 pinch of sea salt
- 1 ounce (30 ml) of water
- 2 tablespoons raw cocoa powder (mix it in half the dough)

*The Swirl*

- 1 tablespoon peanut butter
- 1 teaspoon agave syrup

*End Mix*

- 3 tablespoons of raisins, dipped in rum
- 4 chopped figs

## Preparation

1   Soak the raisins in rum (not mandatory). (Of course, discard rum from children's containers). Soak the cashews in water for 2 to 2.5 hours. Rinse and drain.

2   Enter the dough ingredients (except cocoa powder) in the blender. Mix them until a uniform dough forms.

---

3   Now, put half of the mixture in a bowl and add the cocoa powder to the remaining half in the blender.

4   Mix half of the raisins and chopped figs in the brown dough and the other half in the white dough.

5   Prepare the swirl by mixing peanut butter (at room temperature) and agave syrup.

6   Now, start compiling the containers. Put the brown and white dough in the bowls in turns. Add small balls of butter mixture everywhere.

7   When you reach the last layer, add about 5 peanut butter balls on top. Now, it's all about your creativity and artistic skills. Take a sushi stick and make some cute swirls on top of the dessert.

8   Place the desserts in the fridge for a few hours. Cover the containers with foil if you need to keep them longer.

# Christmas nut cake with ginger

## Ingredient
*MASS MIX*

- ½ cup unroasted buckwheat
- ½ cup of millet
- ⅓ cup (80 ml) unsweetened oat milk
- 1 ripe banana
- 1 tablespoon peanut butter
- 1 pinch of sea salt
- ½ teaspoon of turmeric
- ½ to 1 teaspoon of gingerbread spices
- 2 tablespoons baking powder (add them at the end)

*TO COMBINE WITH MIXED MASS*

- ¼ cup chopped hazelnuts
- ¼ cup chopped almonds
- ¼ cup chopped walnuts
- ¼ cup dried apricots, chopped
- ¼ cup raisins dipped in rum
- 5 chopped figs
- ⅛ cup goji berries
- 2 tablespoons grated orange peel or sugary orange peel (use organic)
- ¼ cup 50g (1.8oz) dark chocolate, chopped

**Process**

- Soak millet and buckwheat overnight (or throughout the day) in water in separate containers. Clean and drain them (you can use a strainer).
- Soak the raisins in a mixture of rum and hot water (half and a half) overnight. You can discard the soaking liquid later, or you can replace it with some of the oat milk in the recipe.
- Chop everything that needs to be cut from the second table.
- Heat the oven to 350 ° F (177 ° C) and line a bread pan with baking paper.
- Place the ingredients in the mixed dough, except for the baking powder, in a blender, and mix them until a uniform dough forms. Do not worry; It is supposed to be quite liquid since millet inflates considerably.
- Now, add the baking powder.
- Finally, combine (DO NOT LIQUUS) chopped nuts, dried fruits, and chocolate.
- Pour the dough into a bread pan and bake for 40 to 45 minutes until your Christmas cake is golden brown.
- Let cool before cutting and serving. If you leave the mold on the counter, cover it with a clean dishcloth or foil (loosely) to keep the cake moist.

# CHAPTER 4

# Mediterranean snacks recipes

**Grilled scallop top in cherry salmorejo**

## Ingredients

- 12 scallops
- 650 gr mature tomatoes
- 350 gr Cherries (I had frozen)
- 200 g milled bread from the day before
- 150 ml extra virgin olive oil Salt to taste
- 1/2 tooth Garlic

## Preparations

1. We are going to make this cherry salmorejo, replacing part of the tomatoes of the classic salmorejo recipe with cherries. It is preferable that you use dark, very ripe cherries that bring a lot of flavors and enough color to the salmorejo, so that the change is noticed (I had a few frozen and boneless)

2. The first thing to do is chop the tomatoes and crush them. If we want to include cucumber in the recipe, we also add it by putting it in the blender glass. Then we will pass the result through a fine strainer, leaving it in a bowl, so it will not be necessary to remove the seeds or peel the tomatoes.

3. As for the cherries, we remove the peduncle and remove the seed with a sharp knife or with a boner. Once we have the pulp of cherries, we crush it and add it to the bowl. Add the sliced bread and let it moisten and soften.

4. Finally, we add the olive oil and optionally half a clove of garlic. Crush the whole and rectify salt.

## Coconut snacks

### Ingredient

- 1 cup pineapple juice
- 2 cups diced mango
- 2 ripe bananas, diced
- ½ vanilla branch
- 4 cups shredded coconut
- ¾ cup roasted grated coconut

### Preparation

1. In a small pot, cook pineapple juice, mango, bananas, and vanilla over medium-low heat for 5 minutes.
2. Scrape the seeds of the vanilla branch in the pot and discard the branch; then cook them for two more minutes.
3. Put the ingredients that are in the pot and the 4 cups of grated coconut inside a food processor with an "S" shaped leaf and process them until you get a mixture without lumps, but firm.
4. Let the mixture cool for about 1 to 2 hours, then, using a small scoop for ice cream or a spoon, place a small amount in your hands and make a ball before rolling it over the toasted coconut.
5. Repeat the process until all your coconut snacks are rolled, I bet you can't eat just one!

# Cucumber and kale open sandwich

## Ingredient

- 2 slices of whole-grain bread, toasted
- 2 to 3 tablespoons of hummus prepared without tahini or oil
- 1 chopped green onion
- ¼ cup chopped fresh cilantro
- 2 medium kale leaves, chopped into small bite-sized pieces (about the size of coriander leaves)
- ½ small cucumber
- Mustard of your choice
- Lemon pepper ( Mrs. Dash and Frontier brands have no salt)

## Preparation

1. Spread hummus generously on toasted bread. Sprinkle the green onion, cilantro, and kale evenly over the hummus.
2. Slice the cucumber in 8 circles and spread each with a thin layer of mustard.
3. Place the cucumber slices, with the mustard down, on top of the coriander and kale layer and press down, if necessary, so that they remain in place.
4. Sprinkle the open sandwich generously with lemon pepper, cut it in half or quarters, if desired, and serve.

# Baked zucchini in cheese breading with aioli sauce

## Recipe

*Zucchini:*

- 2 medium zucchini
- 2 eggs
- ⅓ cup grated parmesan
- 1 tbsp almond flour
- 1/4 tsp garlic powder
- 1 tsp dry parsley
- ½ tsp sea salt
- 1/4 tsp black pepper

*Aioli sauce:*

- 1/4 cup low-carb mayonnaise
- 1 clove of garlic
- 1 tsp fresh lemon juice
- 1/4 tsp black pepper
- A pinch of sea salt

## Cooking

1. Preheat the oven to 204 degrees.
2. Cut the zucchini into strips.
3. Beat the eggs in a medium bowl.
4. In a separate bowl, mix grated parmesan, almond flour, garlic powder, dried parsley, sea salt, and black pepper.

5. Dip slices of zucchini in beaten eggs, and then in the cheese-almond mixture.

6. Place the coated slices on a wire rack placed on a baking sheet. Leave in the preheated oven for 20-25 minutes until they turn golden.

7. In a small bowl, mix all the ingredients for aioli.

8. Remove the zucchini from the oven and serve immediately.

# Stuffed Eggs with Cheese and Olives

## Recipe

- 4 eggs
- 3 tbsp sour cream
- 1 tsp mustard
- 33.75 g black olives (finely chopped)
- 33.75 g blue cheese (crumbled)
- 1/4 tsp sea salt
- 1/8 tsp black pepper
- 1 tsp finely chopped dill, for garnish

## Cooking

1. Put the eggs in a pot of cold water and bring to a boil. Cook for 10-12 minutes, and then clean them.
2. Hard-boiled eggs, cut in half lengthwise, remove the yolks in a bowl and soften them with a fork.
3. In the same bowl, add sour cream, mustard, sea salt and black pepper, and mix well until a creamy condition is obtained.
4. Add finely chopped olives and crumbled blue cheese.
5. Fill the egg whites with the prepared mixture using a pastry bag or bag / rolled parchment with a hole.
6. Arrange the boiled eggs on a plate, garnish with chopped dill and serve.

## Apple "Halloween" lamps

### What you will need

- 6 red apples
- 1 cup peanut butter
- 1 tablespoon date paste
- ½ teaspoon of pumpkin pie spice
- 1 cup of oil-free granola

### Process

1  Preheat the oven to 300-350 ° F (177 ° C).

2  Cut the top of each apple.

3  Take out the inside with a spoon or a melon. Make sure the walls are thick.

4  Carefully carve the face of the flashlight to make eyes and mouth.

5  Melt peanut butter in a saucepan until smooth and smooth.

6  In a bowl, combine melted peanut butter with date paste and pumpkin spices.

7  Fill the apples with the peanut butter mixture and replace the apple tops.

8  Bake the apples on a baking sheet for 10 minutes.

9  Place the granola in the apples and bake for another 10 minutes.

10  Serve immediately.

# Mediterranean recipe of toasted chickpeas

## Ingredients

- 15-ounce cans of chickpeas
- tablespoons of extra virgin olive oil
- teaspoons of red wine vinegar
- 2 teaspoons of fresh lemon juice
- 1 teaspoon kosher salt
- 1 teaspoon dried oregano
- 1/2 teaspoon garlic powder
- 1/2 teaspoon broken black pepper

## Manual

1   Preheat the oven to 425 degrees and line a parchment paper baking sheet. Drain the chickpeas, rinse and dry thoroughly, then lay them in a layer on the baking sheet.

2   Roast for 10 minutes, then take out of the oven, turn the chickpeas with a spatula so that they bake evenly, and then roast for another 10 minutes.

3   Place the remaining ingredients in a large mixing bowl and whisk. Stir in the hot chickpeas and shake gently back and forth until completely covered.

4   Put the coated chickpeas back on the baking sheet and roast for another 10 minutes. Occasionally make sure that they do not overcook and burn. Let yourself cool down and enjoy it!

### Bean salad

**Ingredients**

- 1 pound 15 bean soup mix, dry bean mix
- 1 liter of grapes or cherry tomatoes, halved
- 1 cup of fresh or frozen corn
- 3/4 cup diced red pepper
- 1/2 cup diced red onion
- 1/2 cup chopped shallots
- 1/4 cup chopped parsley or cilantro
- 1/4 cup of olive oil
- spoons of balsamic vinegar
- tablespoons of rice vinegar
- 1 tbsp honey
- 1 tablespoon of Dijon mustard
- 1/2 teaspoon ground cumin
- salt and pepper

**Instructions**

1. The bean mix bag is opened and the seasoning pack discarded, if included. Soak and cook the beans as indicated on the box. Drain into a large bowl and put it in it.
2. While the beans cool, whisk the olive oil together in a small bowl, all tablespoons of vinegar, honey, mustard, cumin, 1 teaspoon salt and 1/2 teaspoon ground black pepper. Deposit aside.

3    Pour over the beans, all the chopped vegetables and herbs. Drizzle with the vinaigrette, then toss to cover well. Good taste, then salt and pepper if necessary. Cover and refrigerate until ready for serving.

## Spicy red lentil dip.

### Ingredients

- 1 cup of collected and rinsed red lentils
- teaspoons of curry powder
- 1 teaspoon onion powder
- 1 teaspoon of sea salt
- 1/4 teaspoon black pepper
- 1/4 teaspoon turmeric
- 1/2 teaspoon of Garam Masala
- 1/2 teaspoon cumin
- Crackers to serve

### Preparations

1. Put the red lentils and enough water in a saucepan to cover them 1 inch.
2. Bring to boil, then heat down to medium heat.
3. Let cook until soft, for 15-20 minutes.
4. If you still have water left, drain it.
5. Crush the lentils with a fork (they should be quite soft already).
6. Pour in the spices and whisk.
7. Warmly serve with crackers.

## Coconut Bars with Nuts

### Recipe

- 60 g macadamia nuts
- 125 g almond oil
- 54.5 g coconut oil
- 6 tbsp unsweetened grated coconut
- 20 drops of stevia

### Cooking

1 Grind macadamia nuts using a food processor or manually
2 Combine almond oil, coconut oil and grated coconut. Add macadamia nuts and stevia drops.
3 Thoroughly mix and pour the dough into a baking dish lined with parchment paper.
4 Refrigerate overnight, and then cut into pieces.

## Spinach Cheese Bread

### Ingredients

- 225 g almond flour
- 2 tsp baking powder
- ½ tsp salt
- 100 g soft butter
- 85 g fresh spinach, chopped
- 1 clove garlic, finely chopped
- 1 tbsp chopped rosemary
- 2 large eggs
- 140 g grated cheddar cheese

### Cooking

1 Preheat the oven to 200 degrees.
2 Put the almond flour, baking powder and salt in a large bowl. Mix well, then add oil and mix again.
3 Add the remaining ingredients (if you wish, you can leave a little cheddar for the top of the bread). Mix well.
4 Put the dough in a cast-iron skillet, greased with oil, and form a pancake with a thickness of about 3.5-4 cm.
5 Bake for 25-30 minutes; then leave the bread in the pan for 15 minutes to cool.

## Roasted Chickpeas

### Ingredient

- 2 cans of 15 ounces (425 g) of chickpeas, rinsed and drained
- 1 teaspoon garlic powder
- 2 teaspoons chili powder
- ½ teaspoon of sea salt
- 2 tablespoons lemon juice

### Process

1 Preheat the oven to 400 ° F (200 ° C). Line a baking sheet with parchment paper and set it aside.

2 Place the chickpeas in a one-gallon (liter) sealed plastic bag and add seasonings. Shake well until completely covered.

3 Spread spicy chickpeas evenly over the prepared baking sheet.

4 Bake for 45 to 55 minutes, stirring every 15 to 20 minutes so that the chickpeas cook evenly, until golden brown.

5 Serve hot or cold for a snack at any time.

## Almond butter toast with sweet potatoes and blueberries

### Ingredient

- 1 sweet potato, sliced half a centimeter thick
- ¼ cup almond butter
- ½ cup blueberries

### Preparation

1 Preheat the oven to 350-360 ° F (177 ° C).

2 Place the sweet potato slices on baking paper. Bake until soft, approximately 20 minutes. (You can also cook them in a toaster, but you would need to activate it at high temperature for three or four cycles).

3 Serve hot, coat with peanut butter and cranberries. Store any leftover sweet potato slices, without dressings, in an airtight container inside the refrigerator for a week. Reheat them in a toaster or in a toaster oven and cover them as instructed

# CONCLUSION

The Mediterranean diet is not exactly a diet, but a diet. In the Mediterranean diet there is no calorie count, no fasting and no elimination of whole food groups. The main idea is good balance and moderation. Balance your food intake well and emphasize those that can be consumed in abundance. Don't overdo it - prepare small portions and consume in moderation. Everyone should think about how the Mediterranean diet can best be tailored to their lifestyle and personal taste. Focus your menu on the foods this diet contains and focus on the foods you like the most. Sweet treats are not excluded, but it is desirable that they are consumed less frequently and in smaller quantities.

Be physically active by aiming for at least 30 minutes a day or 150 minutes a week. Maintain a healthy weight. Drink alcohol in moderation and give up cigarettes.

CPSIA information can be obtained
at www.ICGtesting.com
Printed in the USA
LVHW100907120521
686911LV00040B/602/J

9 781801 839686